AN ANTHOLOGY OF POEMS AND PROSE

AND PROSE

Childhood

ILLUSTRATED WITH PHOTOGRAPHS FROM
THE FRANCIS FRITH COLLECTION

Chosen and edited by
Terence and Eliza Sackett

First published in the United Kingdom in 2003 by
Black Horse Books (an imprint of the Frith Book Company)

This revised and updated edition published by
the Frith Book Company in 2005

British Library Cataloguing in Publication Data
An Anthology of Childhood Poems and Prose
Chosen and edited by Terence and Eliza Sackett
ISBN 1-84589-001-9

Although the publishers have tried to contact all copyright holders before
publication, this has not proved possible in every case. If notified, the
publisher will be pleased to make any necessary arrangements.

Frith Book Company
Frith's Barn, Teffont,
Salisbury, Wiltshire SP3 5QP
Tel: +44 (0) 1722 716 376
Email: info@francisfrith.co.uk
www.francisfrith.co.uk

Front Cover: **WHITBY**, *'Gemini' 1891* 28862p

*The colour-tinting is for illustrative purposes only,
and is not intended to be historically accurate*

Printed and bound in England

Contents

Piping Down the Valleys Wild

PIPING down the valleys wild,
Piping songs of pleasant glee,
On a cloud I saw a child,
And he laughing said to me:

'Pipe a song about a Lamb!'
So I piped with merry cheer.
'Piper, pipe that song again;'
So I piped: he wept to hear.

'Drop thy pipe, thy happy pipe;
Sing thy songs of happy cheer:'
So I sung the same again,
While he wept with joy to hear.

'Piper, sit thee down and write
In a book that all may read.'
So he vanished from my sight,
And I plucked a hollow reed,

And I made a rural pen,
And I stained the water clear,
And I wrote my happy songs
Every child may joy to hear.

WILLIAM BLAKE (1757-1827)
from Songs of Innocence

To an Unborn Infant

BE STILL, sweet babe, no harm shall reach thee,
Nor hurt thy yet unfinished form;
Thy mother's frame shall safely guard thee
From this bleak, this beating storm.

Promised hope! expected treasure!
Oh, how welcome to these arms!
Feeble, yet they'll fondly clasp thee,
Shield thee from the least alarms.

Loved already, little blessing,
Kindly cherished, though unknown,
Fancy forms thee sweet and lovely,
Emblem of the rose unblown …

Start not, babe! the hour approaches
That presents the gift of life;
Soon, too soon, thou'lt taste of sorrow
In these realms of care and strife.

Share not thou a mother's feelings,
Hope vouchsafes a pitying ray;
Though a gloom obscures the morning,
Bright may shine the rising day …

ISABELLA KELLY (1759?-1857)

Song

OH, BABY, baby, baby dear,
We lie alone together here;
The snowy gown and cap and sheet
With lavender are fresh and sweet;
Through half-closed blinds the roses peer
To see and love you, baby dear.

You are so tired, we like to lie
Just doing nothing, you and I,
Within the darkened quiet room.
The sun sends dusk rays through the gloom,
Which is no gloom since you are here,
My little life, my baby dear.

Soft sleepy mouth so vaguely pressed
Against your new-made mother's breast.
Soft little hands in mine I fold,
Soft little feet I kiss and hold,
Round soft smooth head and tiny ear,
All mine, my own, my baby dear …

E NESBIT (1858-1924)

II

Infant Sorrow

MY MOTHER groaned! my father wept.
Into the dangerous world I leapt:
Helpless, naked, piping loud:
Like a fiend hid in a cloud.

Struggling in my father's hands,
Striving against my swaddling bands,
Bound and weary I thought best
To sulk upon my mother's breast.

WILLIAM BLAKE (1757-1827)

First Smiles

A CHILD'S mirth when it at last begins is his first secret; you understand little of it. The first smile (for the convulsive movement in sleep that is popularly adorned by that name is not a smile) is an uncertain sketch of a smile, unpractised but unmistakable. It is accompanied by a single sound—a sound that would be a monosyllable if it were articulate—which is the utterance, though hardly the communication, of a private jollity. That and that alone is the real beginning of human laughter.

From the end of the first fortnight of life, when it appears for the first time, and as it were, flickeringly, the child's smile begins to grow definite, and gradually more frequent. By very slow degrees the secrecy passes away, and the dryness becomes more genial. The child now smiles more openly, but he is still very unlike the laughing creature of so much prose and verse. His laughter takes a long time to form. The monosyllable grows louder, and then comes to be repeated with little catches of his breath. The humour upon which he learns to laugh is that of a human face which approaches him quickly and then withdraws. This is the first intelligible jest of jesting man.

ALICE MEYNELL (1847-1922)

Infant Joy

'I HAVE no name:
I am but two days old.'
What shall I call thee?
'I happy am,
Joy is my name.'
Sweet joy befall thee!

Pretty joy!
Sweet joy but two days old.
Sweet joy I call thee:
Thou dost smile,
I sing the while,
Sweet joy befall thee!

WILLIAM BLAKE (1757-1827)

from Frost at Midnight

DEAR Babe, that sleepest cradled by my side,
Whose gentle breathings, heard in this deep calm,
Fill up the interspersed vacancies
And momentary pauses of the thought!
My babe so beautiful! it thrills my heart
With tender gladness, thus to look at thee,
And think that thou shall learn far other lore,
And in far other scenes! For I was reared
In the great city, pent 'mid cloisters dim,
And saw nought lovely but the sky and stars.
But thou, my babe! shalt wander like a breeze
By lakes and sandy shores, beneath the crags
Of ancient mountain, and beneath the clouds,
Which image in their bulk both lakes and shores
And mountain crags: so shalt thou see and hear
The lovely shapes and sounds intelligible
Of that eternal language, which thy God
Utters, who from eternity doth teach
Himself in all, and all things in himself.
Great universal Teacher! he shall mould
Thy spirit, and by giving make it ask.

Therefore all seasons shall be sweet to thee,
Whether the summer clothe the general earth

With greenness, or the redbreast sit and sing
Betwixt the tufts of snow on the bare branch
Of mossy apple-tree, while the nigh thatch
Smokes in the sun-thaw; whether the eave-drops fall
Heard only in the trances of the blast,
Or if the secret ministry of frost
Shall hang them up in silent icicles,
Quietly shining to the quiet Moon.

SAMUEL TAYLOR COLERIDGE (1772-1834)

The Cottager to her Infant

THE DAYS are cold, the nights are long,
The Northwind sings a doleful song;
Then hush again upon my breast;
All merry things are now at rest,
Save thee, my pretty love!

The kitten sleeps upon the hearth;
The crickets long have ceased their mirth;
There's nothing stirring in the house
Save one wee, hungry, nibbling mouse,
Then why so busy thou?

Nay! start not at the sparkling light;
'Tis but the moon that shines so bright
On the window-pane bedropped with rain:
There, little darling! sleep again,
And wake when it is day.

DOROTHY WORDSWORTH (1771-1855)

Men are Handy wi' Children

'EH, TO be sure,' said Dolly, gently. 'I've seen men as are wonderful handy wi' children. The men are awk'ard and contrary mostly, God help 'em—but when the drink's out of 'em, they aren't unsensible, though they're bad for leeching and bandaging—so fiery and unpatient. You see this goes first, next the skin,' proceeded Dolly, taking up the little shirt, and putting it on.
'Yes,' said Marner, docilely, bringing his eyes very close, that they might be initiated in the mysteries, whereupon Baby seized his head with both her small arms, and put her lips against his face with purring noises.
'See there,' said Dolly, with a woman's tender tact, 'she's fondest o' you. She wants to go o' your lap, I'll be bound. Go, then: take her, Master Marner; you can put the things on, and then you can say as you've done for her from the first of her coming to you.'
Marner took her on his lap, trembling with an emotion mysterious to himself, at something unknown dawning on his life. Thought and feeling were so confused within him, that if he had tried to give them utterance, he could only have said that the child was come instead of the gold—that the gold had turned into the child. He took the
garments from Dolly, and put them on under her teaching; interrupted, of course, by Baby's gymnastics.

GEORGE ELIOT (1819-1880)
from Silas Marner

The Baby

THERE he lay upon his back,
The yearling creature, warm and moist with life
To the bottom of his dimples,—to the ends
Of the lovely tumbled curls about his face;
For since he had been covered over-much
To keep him from the light-glare, both his cheeks
Were hot and scarlet as the first live rose
The shepherd's heart-blood ebbed away into,
The faster for his love. And love was here
As instant; in the pretty baby-mouth,
Shut close as if for dreaming that it sucked,
The little naked feet, drawn up the way
Of nestled birdlings; everything so soft
And tender,—to the tiny holdfast hands,
Which, closing on a finger into sleep,
Had kept the mould of't.
While we stood there dumb,
For oh, that it should take such innocence
To prove just guilt, I thought, and stood there dumb;
The light upon his eyelids pricked them wide,
And staring out at us with all their blue,
As half perplexed between the angelhood
He had been away to visit in his sleep,
And our most mortal presence,—gradually
He saw his mother's face, accepting it

In change for heaven itself, with such a smile
As might have well been learnt there,—never moved,
But smiled on, in a drowse of ecstasy,
So happy (half with her and half with heaven)
He could not have the trouble to be stirred,
But smiled and lay there. Like a rose, I said:
As red and still indeed as any rose,
That blows in all the silence of its leaves,
Content, in blowing, to fulfil its life.
She leaned above him (drinking him as wine)
In that extremity of love, 'twill pass
For agony or rapture, seeing that love
Includes the whole of nature, rounding it
To love … no more,—since more can never be
Than just love. Self-forgot, cast out of self,
And drowning in the transport of the sight,
Her whole pale passionate face, mouth, forehead, eyes,
One gaze, she stood! then, slowly as he smiled,
She smiled too, slowly, smiling unaware,
And drawing from his countenance to hers
A fainter red, as if she watched a flame
And stood in it a-glow. 'How beautiful!'
Said she.

ELIZABETH BARRETT BROWNING (1806-1861)
from Aurora Leigh

The Lamb

LITTLE Lamb, who made thee?
Dost thou know who made thee?
Gave thee life, and bid thee feed
By the stream and o'er the mead;
Gave thee clothing of delight,
Softest clothing, woolly, bright;
Gave thee such a tender voice,
Making all the vales rejoice?
Little Lamb, who made thee?
Dost thou know who made thee?

Little Lamb, I'll tell thee,
Little Lamb, I'll tell thee:
He is called by thy name,
For he calls himself a Lamb.
He is meek, and he is mild,
He became a little child.
I, a child, and thou a lamb,
We are called by his name.
Little Lamb, God bless thee!
Little Lamb, God bless thee!

WILLIAM BLAKE (1757-1827)

Sweet Gipsy Lizzie

GIPSY Lizzie has been put into my reading class. How is the indescribable beauty of that most lovely face to be described—the dark soft curls parting back from the pure white transparent brow, the exquisite little mouth and pearly tiny teeth, the pure straight delicate features, the long dark fringes and white eyelids that droop over and curtain her eyes, when they are cast down or bent upon her book, and seem to rest upon the soft clear cheek, and when the eyes are raised, that clear unfathomable blue depth of wide wonder and enquiry and unsullied and unsuspecting innocence. Oh, child, child, if you did but know your own power. Oh, Gipsy, if you only grow up as good as you are fair. Oh, that you might grow up good. May all God's angels guard you, sweet. The Lord bless thee and keep thee. The Lord make His Face to shine upon thee and be gracious unto thee. The Lord lift up His countenance upon thee and bring thee peace, both now and evermore.

THE REV FRANCIS KILVERT (1840-1879)
from Kilvert's Diary, July 1870

On My Own Little Daughter

SWEET lovely infant, innocently gay,
With blooming face arrayed in peaceful smiles,
How light thy cheerful heart doth sportive play,
Unconscious of all future cares and toils.

With what delight I've seen thy little feet
Dancing with pleasure at my near approach!
Eager they ran my well-known form to meet,
Secure of welcome, fearless of reproach.

Then happy hast thou prattled in mine ear
Thy little anxious tales of pain or joy;
Thy fears lest faithful Tray thy frock should tear,
Thy pride when ladies give the gilded toy …

E'en now methinks I hear the artless tongue,
Lisping sweet sounds of comfort to mine ear:
'Oh, fret no more—your Fanny is not gone—
She will not go—don't cry—your Fanny's here' …

O heavenly Father, guard my infant child;
Protect her steps through this wide scene of care;
Within her breast implant each virtue mild,
And teach her all she ought to hope or fear.

ANON

O This is No' My Ain Bairn

O THIS is no' my ain bairn,
I ken by the greetie o't!
They've changed it for some fairy elf
Aye kicking wi' the feetie o't!
A randy, roaring, cankert thing,
That nought will do but fret and fling,
And gar the very rigging ring
Wi' raging at the meatie o't!

This canna be my ain bairn,
That was so gude and bonnie, O!
Wi' dimpled cheek and merry een,
And pawky tricks sae mony, O!
That danced upon her daddy's knee,
Just like a birdie bound to flee,
And aye had kisses sweet to gi'e
A' round about to ony, O!

O yes, it is my ain bairn!
She's coming to hersel' again!
Now blessings on my ain bairn,
She's just my bonnie Bell again!
Her merry een, her rosy mou',
Ance mair wi' balmy kisses fu'—
I kent the bonnie bairn would rue,
And soon would be hersel' again.

ALEXANDER SMART

Baby Marion

TWO EYES of bonniest, brightest blue,
Has she,—my Baby Marion;
And locks the sunlight glances through
In glee, has Baby Marion.

But, ah! I cannot further go
In praise, my Baby Marion,
If honestly I mean to show
Your ways, my Baby Marion!

Your face with soot from off the grate
Is blacked, my Baby Marion;
Stern truth compels me here to state
The fact, my Baby Marion.

And all unshod is one wee foot—
O sad, sad Baby Marion!
The other has nor sock nor boot—
Oh, bad, bad Baby Marion.

That sockless foot, so dark of hue,
Declares, my Baby Marion,
What devious ways you've travelled through
Upstairs, my Baby Marion.

Through wet it's wandered—been in dust—
In soot, my Baby Marion;
Nay, has a tinge that looks like rust,
To boot, my Baby Marion.

Those hands! that pinafore! ah, me!
'Tis plain, my Baby Marion,
Example, precept—all for thee
Are vain, my Baby Marion.

And do you claim, with childish grace,
A kiss, my Baby Marion?
With hands—with pinafore—with face—
Like this, my Baby Marion? …

But come with dusty hands and face
To me, my Baby Marion;
Assume your own, your rightful place—
My knee, my Baby Marion!

Forget this small unpleasantness
In sleep, my Baby Marion;
And I will pray good angels bless
And keep my Baby Marion.

ELLEN CORBET NICHOLSON

What can be the Matter with Sarah?

ONE DAY some of the schoolchildren came rushing into the School house to tell Mr Evans that Sarah Chard Cooper, the gardener's little granddaughter, was running about the school as if she were mad and they could not stop her. The children added that they believed Sarah was drunk. Mr Evans went out immediately to see what was the matter and he found the little girl running wildly round and round the school with her hair streaming, and her eyes glaring and starting out of her head. They could not stop her, she slipped through their hands and rushed past them, running round in circles plainly quite beside herself. It was true the child was drunk. Her grandmother Mrs Cooper confessed afterwards laughing that she had been drinking brandy herself and had given the child some.

THE REV FRANCIS KILVERT (1840-1879)
from Kilvert's Diary, February 1872

A Terrible Infant

I RECOLLECT a nurse called Ann
Who carried me about the grass,
And one fine day a fine young man
Came up, and kissed the pretty lass.
She did not make the least objection!
Thinks I, 'Aha!
When I can talk I'll tell Mamma.'
—And that's my earliest recollection.

FREDERICK LOCKER-LAMPSON (1821-1895)

The River's Song

CLEAR and cool, clear and cool
By laughing shallow, and dreaming pool;
Cool and clear, cool and clear,
By shining shingle, and foaming weir;
Under the crag where the ouzel sings,
And the ivied wall where the church-bell rings,
Undefiled, for the undefiled;
Play by me, bathe in me, mother and child.

Dank and foul, dank and foul,
By the smoky town in its murky cowl;
Foul and dank, foul and dank,
By wharf and sewer and slimy bank;
Darker and darker the farther I go,
Baser and baser the richer I grow;
Who dares sport with the sin-defiled?
Shrink from me, turn from me, mother and child.

Strong and free, strong and free,
The floodgates are open, away to the sea,
Free and strong, free and strong,
Cleansing my streams as I hurry along,
To the golden sands, and the leaping bar,
And the taintless tide that awaits me afar.

As I lose myself in the infinite main,
Like a soul that has sinned and is pardoned again.
Undefiled, for the undefiled;
Play by me, bathe in me, mother and child.

CHARLES KINGSLEY (1819-1875)
from The Water Babies

Playing In the Farmyard

IN THE coldest weather one or more of the labourer's children are sure to be found in the farmyard somewhere. After the mother has dressed her boy (who may be about three or four years old) in the morning, he is at once turned out of doors to take care of himself, and if, as is often the case, the cottage is within a short distance of the farmyard, thither he toddles directly. He stands about the stable door, watching the harnessing of the great cart-horses, which are, from the very first, the object of his intense admiration …
When the horses are gone … he may be met with round the hay-ricks, dragging a log of wood by a piece of tar cord, the log representing a plough … He looks up at you with half-frightened, half-curious gaze, and mouth open. His hat is an old one of his father's, a mile too big, coming down over his ears to his shoulders, well greased from ancient use—a thing not without its advantage, since it makes it impervious to rain. He wears … a pair of stumping boots, the very picture in miniature of his father's, heeled and tipped with iron. His naked legs are red with the cold, but thick and strong; his cheeks are plump and firm, his round blue eyes bright, his hair almost white, like bleached straw.
An hour or two ago his skin was clean enough, for he was sent out well washed, but is now pretty well grimed, for he has been making himself happy in the dirt, as a boy should do if he be a boy … Once

during the day he may perhaps steal round the farmhouse, and peer wistfully from behind the tubs or buckets into the kitchen, when, if the mistress chances to be about, he is pretty certain to pick up some trifle in the edible line.

RICHARD JEFFERIES (1848-1887)
from Hodge and His Masters

Nurse's Song

WHEN the voices of children are heard on the green
And laughing is heard on the hill,
My heart is at rest within my breast
And everything else is still.

'Then come home, my children, the sun is gone down
And the dews of night arise;
Come, come, leave off play, and let us away
Till the morning appears in the skies.'

'No, no, let us play, for it is yet day
And we cannot go to sleep;
Besides, in the sky the little birds fly
And the hills are all covered with sheep.'

'Well, well, go and play till the light fades away
And then go home to bed.'
The little ones leaped and shouted and laughed
And all the hills echoed.

WILLIAM BLAKE (1757-1827)
from Songs of Innocence

Two Little Figures in the Dusk

IN THE Common Field in front of the cottages I found two little figures in the dusk. One tiny urchin was carefully binding a handkerchief round the face of an urchin even more tiny than himself. It was Fred and Jerry Savine. 'What are you doing to him?' I asked Fred. 'Please, Sir,' said the child solemnly. 'Please, Sir, we'm gwine to play at blindman's buff.' The two children were quite alone. The strip of dusky meadow was like a marsh and every footstep trod the water out of the soaked land, but the two little images went solemnly on with their game as if they were in a magnificent playground with a hundred children to play with. Oh, the wealth of a child's imagination and capacity for enjoyment of trifles.

THE REV FRANCIS KILVERT (1840-1879)
from Kilvert's Diary, January 1875

Fun and Frolics on the Beach

THERE are certain spots on the beach where people crowd together. This is one of them; just west of the West Pier there is a fair between eleven and one every bright morning. Everybody goes because everybody else does. Mamma goes down to bathe with her daughters and the little ones; they take two machines at least; the pater comes to smoke his cigar; the young fellows of the family-party come to look at 'the women', as they irreverently speak of the sex. So the story runs on ad infinitum, down to the shoeless ones that turn up everywhere. Every seat is occupied; the boats and small yachts are filled; some of the children pour pebbles into the boats, some carefully throw them out; wooden spades are busy; sometimes they knock each other on the head with them, sometimes they empty pails of sea-water on a sister's frock. There is a squealing, squalling, screaming, shouting, singing, bawling, howling, whistling, tin-trumpeting, and every luxury of noise.

RICHARD JEFFERIES (1848-1887)
from The Open Air

Letty's Globe

WHEN Letty had scarce passed her third glad year,
And her young, artless words began to flow,
One day we gave the child a coloured sphere
Of the wide earth, that she might mark and know,
By tint and outline, all its sea and land.
She patted all the world; old empires peeped
Between her baby fingers; her soft hand
Was welcome at all frontiers. How she leaped.
And laughed, and prattled in her world-wide bliss;
But when we turned her sweet unlearned eye
On our own isle, she raised a joyous cry,
'Oh! yes, I see it, Letty's home is there!'
And, while she hid all England with a kiss,
Bright over Europe fell her golden hair.

CHARLES TENNYSON TURNER (1808-1879)

Laughter and Tears

THE FAMILY gatherings were the brightest hours in the day, lit up as they were with his marvellous humour. Bright—not only because of the joy his great heart took in his nearest and dearest—but bright on the Bible principle—that 'a merry heart is a continual feast', and sunshine necessary to the development and actual health and growth of all things, especially the young. 'I wonder,' he would say, 'if there is so much laughing in any other home in England as in ours.' He became a light-hearted boy once more in the presence of his children …

The griefs of children were to him most piteous. 'A child over a broken toy is a sight I cannot bear'; and when nursery griefs and broken toys were taken to the study, he was never too busy to mend the toy and dry the tears.

FRANCES KINGSLEY (1814-1891)
from Charles Kingsley: His Letters and Memories of his Life

The Best Education

ALL OF you with little children, and who have no need to count expense, or even if you have such need, take them somehow into the country among green grass and yellow wheat—among trees— by hills and streams, if you wish their highest education, that of the heart and the soul, to be completed.

Therein shall they find a Secret—a knowledge not to be written, not to be found in books. They shall know the sun and the wind, the running water, and the breast of the broad earth. Under the green spray, among the hazel boughs where the nightingale sings, they shall find a Secret, a feeling, a sense that fills the heart with an emotion never to be forgotten. They will forget their books—they will never forget the grassy fields …

They want the unconscious teaching of the country, and without that they will never know the truths of this life. They need to feel— unconsciously—the influence of the air that blows, sun-sweetened, over fragrant hay; to feel the influence of deep shady woods, mile-deep in boughs—the stream—the high hills; they need to revel in long grass. Put away their books, and give them the freedom of the meadows.

RICHARD JEFFERIES (1848-1887)
from The Dewy Morn

A Gloomy Classroom

I GAZED upon the schoolroom into which he took me, as the most forlorn and desolate place I had ever seen. I see it now. A long room, with three long rows of desks, and six of forms, and bristling all round with pegs for hats and slates. Scraps of old copy-books and exercises litter the dirty floor. Some silkworms' houses, made of the same materials, are scattered over the desks. Two miserable little white mice, left behind by their owner, are running up and down in a fusty castle made of pasteboard and wire, looking in all the corners with their red eyes for anything to eat. A bird, in a cage very little bigger than himself, makes a mournful rattle now and then in hopping on his perch, two inches high, or dropping from it; but neither sings nor chirps. There is a strange unwholesome smell upon the room, like mildewed corduroys, sweet apples wanting air, and rotten books. There could not well be more ink splashed about it, if it had been roofless from its first construction, and the skies had rained, snowed, hailed, and blown ink through the varying seasons of the year.

CHARLES DICKENS (1812-1870)
from David Copperfield

Cruel Mr Creakle

I SHOULD think there never can have been a man who enjoyed his profession more than Mr Creakle did. He had a delight in cutting at the boys, which was like the satisfaction of a craving appetite. I am confident that he couldn't resist a chubby boy, especially … I was chubby myself, and ought to know …

Here I sit at the desk again, watching his eye—humbly watching his eye, as he rules a ciphering book for another victim whose hands have just been flattened by that identical ruler, and who is trying to wipe the sting out with a pocket-handkerchief … He makes dreadful mouths as he rules the ciphering book; and now he throws his eye sideways down our lane, and we all droop over our books and tremble. A moment afterwards we are again eyeing him. An unhappy culprit, found guilty of imperfect exercise, approaches at his command. The culprit falters excuses, and professes a determination to do better tomorrow. Mr Creakle cuts a joke before he beats him, and we laugh at it—miserable little dogs, we laugh, with our visages as white as ashes, and our hearts sinking into our boots.

CHARLES DICKENS (1812-1870)
from David Copperfield

An Enlightened Father

HE BUILT for his children as an outdoor nursery, a hut, where they kept books, toys, and tea-things, and spent long happy days; and there he would join them when his parish work was done, bringing them some fresh treasure picked up in his walk, a choice wild flower or fern, or rare beetle, sometimes a lizard or a field-mouse; ever waking up their sense of wonder, and calling out their powers of observation …

Punishment was a thing little known in his house. Corporal punishment was never allowed. His own childish experience of the sense of degradation and unhealthy fear it produced, of the antagonism it called out between a child and its parents, a pupil and his teachers, gave him a horror of it. It had other evils, too, he considered, besides degrading both parties concerned. 'More than half the lying of children,' he said, 'is, I believe, the result of fear, and the fear of punishment.'

FRANCES KINGSLEY (1814-1891)
from Charles Kingsley: His Letters and Memories of his Life

Our Rosie

MRS WIDGER returned with a flat parcel. She undid the string, the children watching with greedy curiosity. She placed on the best-lighted chair an enlargement of a baby's photograph, in a cheap frame, all complete. 'There!' she said.

'What is ut?' asked Tony. 'Why, 'tis li'l Rosie!'

'Wer did 'ee get 'en?' he continued more softly. 'Yu an't had 'en give'd 'ee?'

'Give'd me? No! Thic cheap-jack—but 'tisn' bad, is it?' …

'What did 'ee pay 'en for thic then?'

'Never yu mind. 'Twasn't none o' yours what I paid. What do 'ee think o' it?'

''Tisn' bad—very nice,' remarked Tony, bending before the picture, examining it in all lights. 'Iss; 'tisn' bad by no means. Come yer, Jimmy an' Tommy. Do 'ee know who that ther is?'

'Rosie!' whispered Jimmy.

'What was took up to cementry,' added Tommy in a brighter voice.

'Iss, 'tis our li'l Rosie to the life (mustn' touch), jest like her was' …

The children's riot began again. 'Our Rosie—' they were saying.

Mam 'Idger, slipping out of Tony's grasp, carried the picture off to the front room. She was sometime gone.

Wordsworth's We are Seven came into my mind:

'But they are dead; those two are dead!

Their spirits are in heaven!'

'Twas throwing words away; for still

The little maid would have her will,

And said, 'Nay, we are seven!'

I knew, of course, intellectually, that the poem records more than a child's mere fancy; but never before have I felt its truth, have I been caught up, so to speak, into the atmosphere of the wise, simple souls who are able to rob death of the worst of its sting by refusing to let the dead die altogether, even on earth. Rosie is dead and buried. I perceive also—I perceived, while Tony and the children stood round that picture—that Rosie is still here, in this house, hallowing it a little. The one statement is as much a fact as the other; but how much more delicately intangible, and perhaps how much truer, the second.

STEPHEN REYNOLDS (1881-1919)
from A Poor Man's House

A Schoolboy's Friendship

AT SCHOOL, friendship is a passion. It entrances the being; it tears the soul. All loves of afterlife can never bring its rapture, or its wretchedness; no bliss so absorbing, no pangs of jealousy or despair so crushing and so keen! What tenderness and what devotion; what illimitable confidence, infinite revelations of inmost thoughts; what ecstatic present and romantic future; what bitter estrangements and what melting reconciliations; what scenes of wild recrimination, agitating explanations, passionate correspondence; what insane sensitiveness, and what frantic sensibility; what earthquakes of the heart and whirlwinds of the soul are confined in that simple phrase, a schoolboy's friendship!

BENJAMIN DISRAELI (1804-1881)
from Coningsby

Simple, Commonplace Affections

MY DIFFICULTY is to get rid of the children when I wish to go out by myself. They follow me out to the seafront, and meet me there when I return, running towards me with shouting and arms upraised, tumbling over their own toes, and taking me home as if I were a huge pet dog of theirs. 'Where be yu going?' they ask, and, 'Where yu been?' Jimmy regards me as a fixture. 'When yu goes away for two or dree days,' he says, 'I'll write to 'ee, like Dad du.' I cross the Square, and some child, lolling over the board across a doorway, laughs to me shrilly and waves its arms. If by taking thought, I could send such a glow to the hearts of those I love, as that child, without thinking, sends to mine—but I cannot. I can only wave a hand back to the child, and be thankful and full-hearted. Often enough I wish I could have a piano and find out whether my fingers will still play Chopin, Beethoven, and Bach; often I hanker after a sight of a certain picture or a certain statue in the Louvre or Luxembourg, for a concert, a theatre, a right-down good argument on some intellectual point, or for the books I want to read and never shall. Yet, all in all, I am never sorry for long. This children's babble and laughter, these simple, commonplace, wonderful affections, are a hundred times worth everything I miss.

STEPHEN REYNOLDS (1881-1919)
from A Poor Man's House

from I Remember, I Remember

I REMEMBER, I remember,
The house where I was born,
The little window where the sun
Came peeping in at morn;
He never came a wink too soon,
Nor brought too long a day,
But now, I often wish the night
Had borne my breath away!

I remember, I remember
The roses, red and white,
The violets, and the lily-cups—
Those flowers made of light!
The lilacs where the robin built,
And where my brother set
The laburnum on his birth-day,—
The tree is living yet! …

I remember, I remember
The fir trees dark and high;
I used to think their slender tops
Were close against the sky:
It was a childish ignorance,
But now 'tis little joy
To know I'm farther off from Heaven
Than when I was a boy.

THOMAS HOOD (1799-1845)

The Children's Hour

BETWEEN the dark and the daylight,
When the night is beginning to lower,
Comes a pause in the day's occupations,
That is known as the Children's Hour.

I hear in the chamber above me
The patter of little feet,
The sound of a door that is opened,
And voices soft and sweet.

From my study I see in the lamplight,
Descending the broad hall stair,
Grave Alice, and laughing Allegra,
And Edith with golden hair.

A whisper, and then a silence:
Yet I know by their merry eyes
They are plotting and planning together
To take me by surprise.

A sudden rush from the stairway,
A sudden raid from the hall!
By three doors left unguarded,
They enter my castle wall!

They climb up into my turret
O'er the arms and back of my chair;
If I try to escape, they surround me;
They seem to be everywhere.

They almost devour me with kisses,
Their arms about me entwine,
Till I think of the Bishop of Bingen
In his Mouse-Tower on the Rhine!

Do you think, O blue-eyed banditti,
Because you have scaled the wall,
Such an old moustache as I am
Is not a match for you all?

I have you fast in my fortress,
And will not let you depart,
But put you down into the dungeon
In the round-tower of my heart.

And there I shall keep you forever,
Yes, forever and a day,
Till the walls shall crumble to ruin,
And moulder in dust away!

H W LONGFELLOW (1807-1882)

The Lamplighter

MY TEA is nearly ready and the sun has left the sky;
It's time to take the window to see Leerie going by;
For every night at teatime and before you take your seat,
With lantern and with ladder he comes posting up the street.

Now Tom would be a driver and Maria go to sea,
And my papa's a banker and as rich as he can be;
But I, when I am stronger and can choose what I'm to do,
O Leerie, I'll go round at night and light the lamps with you!

For we are very lucky, with a lamp before the door,
And Leerie stops to light it as he lights so many more;
And O! before you hurry by with ladder and with light,
O Leerie, see a little child and nod to him to-night!

ROBERT LOUIS STEVENSON (1850-1894)

To Bronwen

IF I should ever by chance grow rich
I'll buy Codham, Cockridden, and Childerditch,
Roses, Pyrgo, and Lapwater,
And let them all to my elder daughter.
The rent I shall ask of her will be only
Each year's first violets, white and lonely,
The first primroses and orchises—
She must find them before I do, that is.
But if she finds a blossom on furze
Without rent they shall all forever be hers,
Codham, Cockridden, and Childerditch,
Roses, Pyrgo, and Lapwater,—
I shall give them all to my elder daughter.

EDWARD THOMAS (1878-1917)

Shyness Conquered

USUALLY, at breakfast time, the voices of Tony's small nieces may be heard coming down the passage: 'Aunt-ieAnn-ie! Aunt-ieAnn-ie!' Their tousled, tow-coloured little heads peep round the doorway. If we have not yet finished eating, they are promptly ordered to 'get 'long home to mother.' Otherwise, they come right in and remain standing in the middle of the room, apparently to view me. Unable to remember which is Dora and which Dolly, I have nicknamed them according to their hair, Straighty and Curley. What they think of things, there is no knowing; for they blush at direct questions and turn their heads away. So also, when I have been going in and out of the Square, they have stopped their play to gaze at me, but have merely smiled shyly, if at all, in answer to my greetings. Yesterday, however, they had a skipping rope. I jumped over it. Instantly there was a chorus of laughter and chatter. The ice was broken. This morning, after a moment or two's consideration behind her veil of unbrushed hair, Straighty came and clambered upon the arm of the courting chair—dabbed a clammy little hand down my neck, whilst Curley plumped her fist on my knee and stayed looking into my face with very wondering smiling blue eyes. By the simple act of jumping a rope, I had gained their confidence; had proved I was really a fellow creature, I suppose. Now, when I pass through the Square, some small boy is sure to call out, 'Where yu going?' And my name is brandished about among the children as if I were a pet animal. They have appropriated me. They have tamed that mysterious wild beast, 'the gen'leman.'

STEPHEN REYNOLDS (1881-1919)
from A Poor Man's House

To Alison Cunningham From Her Boy

FOR THE long nights you lay awake
And watched for my unworthy sake:
For your most comfortable hand
That led me through the uneven land:
For all the story-books you read:
For all the pains you comforted:
For all you pitied, all you bore,
In sad and happy days of yore:—
My second mother, my first wife,
The angel of my infant life—
From the sick child, now well and old,
Take, nurse, the little book you hold!

And grant it, heaven, that all who read
May find as dear a nurse at need,
And every child who lists my rhyme,
In the bright, fireside, nursery clime,
May hear it in as kind a voice
As made my childish days rejoice!

ROBERT LOUIS STEVENSON (1850-1894)

On the Receipt of My Mother's Picture

O THAT those lips had language! Life has passed
With me but roughly since I heard thee last.
Those lips are thine—thy own sweet smile I see,
The same that oft in childhood solaced me;
Voice only fails, else how distinct they say,
'Grieve not, my child, chase all thy fears away!'
The meek intelligence of those dear eyes
(Blest be the art that can immortalize,
The art that baffles time's Tyrannic claim
To quench it) here shines on me still the same …

My mother! when I learned that thou wast dead,
Say, wast thou conscious of the tears I shed?
Hovered thy spirit o'er thy sorrowing son,
Wretch even then, life's journey just begun?
Perhaps thou gavest me, though unfelt, a kiss;
Perhaps a tear, if souls can weep in bliss—
Ah, that maternal smile! it answers—Yes.
I heard the bell tolled on thy burial day,
I saw the hearse that bore thee slow away,
And, turning from my nursery window, drew
A long, long sigh, and wept a last adieu!
But was it such?—It was.—Where thou art gone
Adieus and farewells are a sound unknown.
May I but meet thee on that peaceful shore,
The parting word shall pass my lips no more! …

Where once we dwelt our name is heard no more,
Children not thine have trod my nursery floor;
And where the gardener Robin, day by day,
Drew me to school along the public way,
Delighted with my bauble coach, and wrapped
In scarlet mantle warm, and velvet capped,
'Tis now become a history little known,
That once we called the pastoral house our own …

And now, farewell—Time unrevoked has run
His wonted course, yet what I wished is done.
By contemplation's help, not sought in vain,
I seem to have lived my childhood o'er again;
To have renewed the joys that once were mine,
Without the sin of violating thine;
And, while the wings of fancy still are free,
And I can view this mimic show of thee,
Time has but half succeeded in his theft—
Thyself removed, thy power to sooth me left.

WILLIAM COWPER (1731-1800)

Mothers' Instincts

WOMEN know
The way to rear up children (to be just),
They know a simple, merry, tender knack
Of tying sashes, fitting baby-shoes,
And stringing pretty words that make no sense,
And kissing full sense into empty words,
Which things are corals to cut life upon,
Although such trifles: children learn by such,
Love's holy earnest in a pretty play
And get not over-early solemnised,
But seeing, as in a rose-bush, Love Divine
Which burns and hurts not,—not a single bloom,—
Become aware and unafraid of Love.
Such good do mothers …

ELIZABETH BARRETT BROWNING (1806-1861)
from Aurora Leigh

The Start of a Busy Day

THE FAMILY cares call next upon the wife
To quit her mean but comfortable bed.
And first she stirs the fire and blows the flame,
Then from her heap of sticks, for winter stored,
An armful brings; loud-crackling as they burn,
Thick fly the red sparks upward to the roof,
While slowly mounts the smoke in wreathy clouds.
On goes the seething pot with morning cheer,
For which some little wishful hearts await,
Who, peeping from the bedclothes, spy well-pleased
The cheery light that blazes on the wall,
And bawl for leave to rise.—
Their busy mother knows not where to turn,
Her morning work comes now so thick upon her.
One she must help to tie his little coat,
Unpin his cap, and seek another's shoe.
When all is o'er, out to the door they run,
With new-combed sleeky hair and glistening cheeks,
Each with some little project in his head.

JOANNA BAILLIE (1762-1851)
from A Winter's Day

How to Get Supper for Nothing

AS THE filled barrows [of pilchards] are going into the salting-house, we observe a little urchin running by the side of them, and hitting their edges with a long cane, in a constant succession of smart strokes, until they are fairly carried through the gate, when he quickly returns to perform the same office for the next series that arrive. The object of this apparently unaccountable proceeding is soon practically illustrated by a group of children, hovering about the entrance of the salting-house, who every now and then dash resolutely up to the barrows, and endeavour to seize on as many fish as they can take away at one snatch. It is understood to be their privilege to keep as many pilchards as they can get in this way by their dexterity, in spite of a liberal allowance of strokes aimed at their hands; and their adroitness richly deserves its reward. Vainly does the boy officially entrusted with the administration of the cane, strike the sides of the barrow with malignant smartness and perseverance—fish are snatched away with lightning rapidity and pick-pocket neatness of hand. The hardest rap over the knuckles fails to daunt the sturdy little assailants. Howling with pain, they dash up to the next barrow that passes them, with unimpaired resolution; and often collect their ten or a dozen fish a piece, in an hour or two.

WILKIE COLLINS (1824-1889)
from Rambles Beyond Railways

A Hungry Child

AS I was sitting in a confectioner's shop eating a bun I saw lingering about the door a barefooted child, a little girl, with fair hair tossed and tangled wild, an arch espiègle eager little face and beautiful wild eyes, large and grey, which looked shyly into the shop and at me with a wistful beseeching smile. She wore a poor faded ragged frock and her shapely limbs and tiny delicate beautiful feet were bare and stained with mud and dust. Still she lingered about the place with her sad and wistful smile and her winning beseeching look, half hiding herself shyly behind the door. It was irresistible. Christ seemed to be looking at me through the beautiful wistful imploring eyes of the barefooted hungry child. I took her out a bun, and I shall never forget the quick happy grateful smile which flashed over her face as she took it and began to eat. She said she was very hungry. Poor lamb. I asked her name and she told me, but amidst the roar of the street and the bustle of the crowded pavement I could not catch the accents of the childish voice. Never mind. I shall know some day.

THE REV FRANCIS KILVERT (1840-1879)
from Kilvert's Diary, June 1874

Spring and Fall: To a Young Child

MARGARET, are you grieving
Over Goldengrove unleaving?
Leaves, like the things of man, you
With your fresh thoughts care for, can you?
Ah! as the heart grows older
It will come to such sights colder
By and by, nor spare a sigh
Though worlds of wanwood leafmeal lie;
And yet you will weep and know why.
Now no matter, child, the name:
Sorrow's springs are the same.
Nor mouth had, no nor mind, expressed
What heart heard of, ghost guessed:
It is the blight man was born for,
It is Margaret you mourn for.

GERARD MANLEY HOPKINS (1844-1889)

The Self-Unseeing

HERE is the ancient floor,
Footworn and hollowed and thin,
Here was the former door
Where the dead feet walked in.

She sat here in her chair,
Smiling into the fire;
He who played stood there,
Bowing it higher and higher.

Childlike, I danced in a dream;
Blessings emblazoned that day;
Everything glowed with a gleam;
Yet we were looking away!

THOMAS HARDY (1840-1928)

Piano

SOFTLY, in the dusk, a woman is singing to me;
Taking me back down the vista of years, till I see
A child sitting under the piano, in the boom of the tingling strings
And pressing the small, poised feet of a mother who smiles as she sings.
In spite of myself, the insidious mastery of song
Betrays me back, till the heart of me weeps to belong
To the old Sunday evenings at home, with winter outside
And hymns in the cosy parlour, the tinkling piano our guide.
So now it is vain for the singer to burst into clamour
With the great black piano appassionato. The glamour
Of childish days is upon me, my manhood is cast
Down in the flood of remembrance, I weep like a child for the past.

D H LAWRENCE (1885-1930)

My Entrance into the World

ALL APPEARED new, and strange at first, inexpressibly rare and delightful and beautiful. I was a little stranger, which at my entrance into the world was saluted and surrounded with innumerable joys. My knowledge was Divine. I knew by intuition those things which since my Apostasy, I collected again by the highest reason. My very ignorance was advantageous. I seemed as one brought into the Estate of Innocence. All things were spotless and pure and glorious: yea, and infinitely mine, and joyful and precious, I knew not that there were any sins, or complaints or laws. I dreamed not of poverties, contentions or vices. All tears and quarrels were hidden from mine eyes. Everything was at rest, free and immortal. I knew nothing of sickness or death or rents or exaction, either for tribute or bread. In the absence of these I was entertained like an Angel with the works of God in their splendour and glory, I saw all in the peace of Eden; Heaven and Earth did sing my Creator's praises, and could not make more melody to Adam, than to me. All Time was Eternity, and a perpetual Sabbath. Is it not strange, that an infant should be heir of the whole World, and see those mysteries which the books of the learned never unfold?

THOMAS TRAHERNE (1636?-1674)
from Centuries of Meditations

The Retreat

HAPPY those early days, when I
Shined in my Angel-infancy!
Before I understood this place
Appointed for my second race,
Or taught my soul to fancy ought
But a white, celestial thought;
When yet I had not walked above
A mile or two from my first Love,
And looking back, at that short space
Could see a glimpse of His bright face;
When on some gilded cloud, or flower
My gazing soul would dwell an hour,
And in those weaker glories spy
Some shadows of eternity;
Before I taught my tongue to wound
My conscience with a sinful sound,
Or had the black art to dispense
A several sin to every sense,
But felt through all this fleshly dress
Bright shoots of everlastingness.

O how I long to travel back,
And tread again that ancient track!
That I might once more reach that plain,

Where first I left my glorious train;
From whence th' enlightened spirit sees
That shady City of Palm trees!
But ah! my soul with too much stay
Is drunk, and staggers in the way:—
Some men a forward motion love,
But I by backward steps would move;
And when this dust falls to the urn,
In that state I came, return.

HENRY VAUGHAN (1622-1695)

In a Garden

BABY, see the flowers!
—Baby sees
Fairer things than these,
Fairer though they be than dreams of ours.

Baby, hear the birds!
—Baby knows
Better songs than those,
Sweeter though they sound than sweetest words.

Baby, see the moon!
—Baby's eyes
Laugh to watch it rise,
Answering light with love and night with noon.

Baby, hear the sea!
—Baby's face
Takes a graver grace,
Touched with wonder what the sound may be.

Baby, see the star!
—Baby's hand
Opens, warm and bland,
Calm in claim of all things fair that are.

Baby, hear the bells!
—Baby's head
Bows, as ripe for bed,
Now the flowers curl round and close their cells.

Baby, flower of light,
—Sleep, and see
Brighter dreams than we,
Till good day shall smile away good night.

ALGERNON CHARLES SWINBURNE (1837-1909)

A Blissful Fullness

WHEN I penetrate backward into my childhood I come perhaps sooner than many people to impassable night. A sweet darkness enfolds with a faint blessing my life up to the age of about four. The task of attempting stubbornly to break up that darkness is one I have never proposed to myself, but I have many times gone up to the edge of it, peering, listening, stretching out my hands, and I have heard the voice of one singing as I sat or lay in her arms; and I have become again aware very dimly of being enclosed in rooms that were shadowy, whether by comparison with outer sunlight I know not. The songs, first of my mother, then of her younger sister, I can hear not only afar off behind the veil but on this side of it also. I was, I think, a very still listener whom the music flowed through and filled to the exclusion of all thought and of all sensation except of blissful easy fullness, so that too early or too sudden ceasing would have meant pangs of expectant emptiness. The one song which, by reason of its repetition or of some aptitude in me, I well remember, was one combining fondness with tranquil if peevish retrospection and regret in a soft heavy twilight. I reach back to it in that effort through a thousand twilights lineally descended from that first one and from the night which gave it birth. If I cried or suffered pain or deprivation in those years nothing remains to star the darkness. Either I asked no question or I had none but sweet answers. I was at peace with life. Indoors, out of the sun, I seem never to have been troubled by heat or cold strong enough to be remembered. But out of doors, somewhere at the verge of the dark years, I can recall more simply and completely than any spent indoors at that time one day above others. I lay in the tall grass and buttercups of a narrow field at the edge of London and saw the sky and nothing but the sky. There was someone near, probably a servant, necessary but utterly insignificant. I was alone and happy to be so, just as indoors I was happy among people and shadows between walls. Was it one day or many? I know of no beginning or end to it; but an end I suppose it had, an age past.

EDWARD THOMAS (1878-1917)

Rowing Below a Lakeland Peak

ONE summer evening … I found
A little boat tied to a willow tree
Within a rocky cave, its usual home.
Straight I unloosed her chain, and stepping in
Pushed from the shore. It was an act of stealth
And troubled pleasure, nor without the voice
Of mountain-echoes did my boat move on;
Leaving behind her still, on either side,
Small circles glittering idly in the moon,
Until they melted all into one track
Of sparkling light. But now, like one who rows,
Proud of his skill, to reach a chosen point
With an unswerving line, I fixed my view
Upon the summit of a craggy ridge,
The horizon's utmost boundary; far above
Was nothing but the stars and the grey sky.
She was an elfin pinnace; lustily
I dipped my oars into the silent lake,
And, as I rose upon the stroke, my boat
Went heaving through the water like a swan;
When, from behind that craggy steep till then
The horizon's bound, a huge peak, black and huge,
As if with voluntary power instinct
Upreared its head. I struck and struck again,
And growing still in stature the grim shape

Towered up between me and the stars, and still,
For so it seemed, with purpose of its own
And measured motion like a living thing,
Strode after me. With trembling oars I turned,
And through the silent water stole my way
Back to the covert of the willow tree;
There in her mooring-place I left my bark,—
And through the meadows homeward went, in grave
And serious mood; but after I had seen
That spectacle, for many days, my brain
Worked with a dim and undetermined sense
Of unknown modes of being; o'er my thoughts
There hung a darkness, call it solitude
Or blank desertion. No familiar shapes
Remained, no pleasant images of trees,
Of sea or sky, no colours of green fields;
But huge and mighty forms, that do not live
Like living men, moved slowly through the mind
By day, and were a trouble to my dreams.

WILLIAM WORDSWORTH (1770-1850)
from The Prelude

A Sense of Mystery

IT WAS not, I think, till my eighth year that I began to be distinctly conscious of something more than this mere childish delight in nature. It may have been there all the time from infancy—I don't know; but when I began to know it consciously it was as if some hand had surreptitiously dropped something into the honeyed cup which gave it at certain times a new flavour … I would go out of my way to meet it, and I used to steal out of the house alone when the moon was at its full, to stand, silent and motionless, near some group of large trees, gazing at the dusky green foliage silvered by the beams; and at such times the sense of mystery would grow until a sensation of delight would change to fear, and the fear increase until it was no longer to be borne, and I would hastily escape to recover the sense of reality and safety indoors, where there was light and company. Yet on the very next night I would steal out again and go to the spot where the effect was strongest, which was usually among … the white acacia trees, which gave the name of Las Acacias to our place. The loose feathery foliage on moonlight nights had a peculiar hoary aspect that made this tree seem more intensely alive than others, more conscious of my presence and watchful of me.

W H HUDSON (1841-1922)

from **Ode On Intimations Of Immortality**

THERE was a time when meadow, grove, and stream,
The earth, and every common sight,
To me did seem
Apparelled in celestial light,
The glory and the freshness of a dream.
It is not now as it hath been of yore;—
Turn wheresoe'er I may,
By night or day,
The things which I have seen I now can see no more.

The rainbow comes and goes,
And lovely is the rose;
The moon doth with delight
Look round her when the heavens are bare;
Waters on a starry night
Are beautiful and fair;
The sunshine is a glorious birth;
But yet I know, where'er I go,
That there hath past away a glory from the earth …

Our birth is but a sleep and a forgetting;
The Soul that rises with us, our life's Star,
Hath had elsewhere its setting,
And cometh from afar;
Not in entire forgetfulness,
And not in utter nakedness,

But trailing clouds of glory do we come
From God, who is our home:
Heaven lies about us in our infancy!
Shades of the prison-house begin to close
Upon the growing Boy,
But he beholds the light, and whence it flows,
He sees it in his joy;
The Youth, who daily farther from the east
Must travel, still is Nature's Priest,
And by the vision splendid
Is on his way attended;
At length the Man perceives it die away,
And fade into the light of common day …

Hence in a season of calm weather
Though inland far we be,
Our souls have sight of that immortal sea
Which brought us hither;
Can in a moment travel thither—
And see the children sport upon the shore,
And hear the mighty waters rolling evermore …

WILLIAM WORDSWORTH (1770-1850)

Orient and Immortal Wheat

THE corn was orient and immortal wheat, which never should be reaped, nor was ever sown. I thought it had stood from everlasting to everlasting. The dust and stones of the street were as precious as gold: the gates were at first the end of the world. The green trees when I saw them first through one of the gates transported and ravished me, their sweetness and unusual beauty made my heart to leap, and almost mad with ecstasy, they were such strange and wonderful things. The Men! O what venerable and reverend creatures did the aged seem! Immortal Cherubims! And young men glittering and sparkling Angels, and maids strange seraphic pieces of life and beauty! Boys and girls tumbling in the street, and playing, were moving jewels. I knew not that they were born or should die; But all things abided eternally as they were in their proper places. Eternity was manifest in the Light of the Day, and something infinite behind everything appeared: which talked with my expectation and moved my desire. The city seemed to stand in Eden, or to be built in Heaven. The streets were mine, the temple was mine, the people were mine, their clothes and gold and silver were mine, as much as their sparkling eyes, fair skins and ruddy faces. The skies were mine, and so were the sun and moon and stars, and all the World was mine; and I the only spectator and enjoyer of it.

THOMAS TRAHERNE (1636?-1674)
from Centuries of Meditations

Cradle Song

O MY deir hert, young Jesus sweit,
Prepare thy creddil in my spreit,
And I shall rock thee in my hert
And never more from thee depart.

But I shall praise thee evermoir
With sangis sweit unto they gloir;
The knees of my hert sall I bow
And sing that richt Balulalow.

ANON

III

Lullaby

UPON my lap my sovereign sits
And sucks upon my breast;
Meantime his love maintains my life
And gives my sense her rest.
Sing lullaby, my little boy,
Sing lullaby, mine only joy!

When thou hast taken thy repast,
Repose, my babe, on me;
So may thy mother and thy nurse
Thy cradle also be.

I grieve that duty doth not work
All that my wishing would;
Because I would not be to thee
But in the best I should.

Yet as I am, and as I may,
I must and will be thine,
Though all too little for thyself
Vouchsafing to be mine.
Sing lullaby, my little boy,
Sing lullaby, mine only joy!

RICHARD ROWLANDS (1565-?1630)

Cradle Song

SLEEP, baby, sleep,
Our cottage vale is deep;
The little lamb is on the green,
With woolly fleece so soft and clean,
Sleep, baby, sleep!

Sleep, baby, sleep,
I would not, would not weep;
The little lamb he never cries,
For bright and happy are his eyes,
Sleep, baby, sleep!

Sleep, baby, sleep,
Down where the woodbines creep;
Be always like the lambs so mild,
A kind, and sweet, and gentle child—
Sleep, baby, sleep!

Sleep, baby, sleep,
Thy rest shall angels keep;
While on the grass the lamb shall feed,
And never suffer want or need,
Sleep, baby, sleep!

ANON
Gloucestershire Lullaby

A Lullaby

WEE wearied Lowrie,
Come to mither's knee
An' I'll rock you like a boatie
On the bonnie simmer sea.

Wee sunburnt Lowrie,
Sairly tired wi' play,
He's been toddlin' wi' the lammie
On the hillside a' the day.

Wee rosy Lowrie,
Noo he's sleepin' soun',
An' the wee pet lamb is lookin'
For his playmate roun' an' roun' ...

Ha! there's wee lammie
Comin' toddlin' in,
An' he sees wee Lowrie sleepin',
Sae he winna mak' a din.

Wee wearied Lowrie's
Noo put to his bed,
An' he's sleepin' aye the sounder
As the westlin' sky grows red.

Wee drookit daisies
On the dewy green,
Is the lammie's sweetest nibble
Ere he gaes to rest at e'een.

Twa bonnie lammies,
May you wake the morn,
An' your life be ae long simmer
That the sweetest flowers adorn.

TOM McEWEN

A Cradle Song

SWEET dreams, form a shade
O'er my lovely infant's head;
Sweet dreams of pleasant streams
By happy, silent, moony beams.

Sweet sleep, with soft down
Weave thy brows an infant crown.
Sweet sleep, Angel mild,
Hover o'er my happy child.

Sweet smiles, in the night
Hover over my delight;
Sweet smiles, Mother's smiles,
All the livelong night beguiles.

Sweet moans, dovelike sighs,
Chase not slumber from thy eyes.
Sweet moans, sweeter smiles,
All the dovelike moans beguiles.

Sleep, sleep, happy child,
All creation slept and smiled;
Sleep, sleep, happy sleep,
While o'er thee thy mother weep …

WILLIAM BLAKE (1757-1827)

117

Golden Slumbers

GOLDEN slumbers kiss your eyes,
Smiles awake you when you rise.
Sleep, pretty wantons, do not cry,
And I will sing a lullaby.
Rock them, rock them, lullaby.

Care is heavy, therefore sleep you.
You are care, and care must keep you.
Sleep, pretty wantons, do not cry,
And I will sing a lullaby.
Rock them, rock them, lullaby.

THOMAS DEKKER (1570-1632)

To Any Reader

AS FROM the house your mother sees
You playing round the garden trees,
So you may see, if you will look
Through the windows of this book,
Another child, far, far away,
And in another garden, play.
But do not think you can at all,
By knocking on the window, call
That child to hear you. He intent
Is all on his play-business bent.
He does not hear; he will not look,
Nor yet be lured out of this book.
For, long ago, the truth to say,
He has grown up and gone away,
And it is but a child of air
That lingers in the garden there.

ROBERT LOUIS STEVENSON (1850-1894)

AGENT
for
PULLARS
DYE WORKS
PERTH